W9-AYK-497

DESIGNERS
in Residence

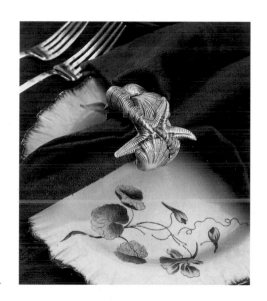

Designers in Residence

The Personal Style of Top Women Decorators and Designers

Text by Claire Whitcomb

Hearst Books

A Division of Sterling Publishing Co., Inc.
New York

Copyright © 2000 by Hearst Communications, Inc.

This book was previously published as a hardcover.

All rights reserved.

Produced by Smallwood & Stewart, Inc.
New York City

Designer Alexandra Maldonado

The Library of Congress has cataloged the hardcover edition as follows:

Designers in residence : the personal style of top women decorators and designers / by the Editors of Victoria Magazine.
      p. cm.
   ISBN 1-58816-003-3
   1. Women interior decorators—Psychology. 2. Interior decoration—History—20th century.
NK2115.3.157 D38 2000
747—dc21
99-086287

10 9 8 7 6 5 4 3 2 1

First Paperback Edition 2005
Published by Hearst Books
A Division of Sterling Publishing Co., Inc.
387 Park Avenue South, New York, NY 10016

Hearst Books is proud to continue the superb style, quality, and tradition of *Victoria* magazine with every book we publish. On our beautifully illustrated pages you will always find inspiration and ideas about the subjects you love.

Victoria is a trademark owned by Hearst Magazines Property, Inc., in USA, and Hearst Communications, Inc., in Canada. Hearst Books is a trademark owned by Hearst Communications, Inc.

For information about custom editions, special sales, premium and corporate purchases, please contact Sterling Special Sales Department at 800-805-5489 or specialsales@sterlingpub.com.

Distributed in Canada by Sterling Publishing
c/o Canadian Manda Group, 165 Dufferin Street
Toronto, Ontario, Canada M6K 3H6

Distributed in Australia by Capricorn Link (Australia) Pty. Ltd.
P.O. Box 704, Windsor, NSW 2756 Australia

Manufactured in China

ISBN 1-58816-497-7

Contents

LABORATORIES OF WHITE

SPACE, CLEVERLY USED

DRAWING ON TRADITION

Foreword

From a 1920s California bungalow to a Harlem apartment, we have found the freshest decorating ideas to share with you. What makes them special is that they all originated in the homes of designers whose work is creating beauty and order for others. But this book shows how these designers choose to live themselves, and it offers a wonderful lexicon for all of us.

What variety we have gathered! Some of our designers are traditional, others innovative. Several take into account busy lives, with children bounding into rooms that seem to take the wear and tear in stride. Others have made home a private retreat in their own unique ways. Some have set apart space for work-at-home environments. You will find both carefully edited rooms and those where collectibles appear to have grown over the fence.

Whatever your own decorating style, you'll discover a kinship in this creative grouping. Each designer has an eye that enables her to make just the right choices, and here she guides your hand in picking fabrics, deciding on accessories, and arranging furniture. In addition, *Designers in Residence* is a series of wonderful stories about women—and about what these women do best. In this book, I think, it is the personal that most instructs and captivates.

Nancy Lindemeyer, Founding Editor
Victoria

Introduction

Before you turn a page, we, the editors of *Victoria*, would like to make a confession: this is not a decorating book. Yes, it's brimming with ideas for window treatments, color schemes, and furniture layouts. Yes, it has tips, trade secrets, advice, and inspiration from some of the design field's most creative women. But a decorating book? No, this is a book about passion: a passion for transforming life's givens—rooms with four walls, furniture with four legs—into homes that are unique, personal, and incredibly rewarding. Decorating is simply a means to an end.

Spend a moment with Christiane Michaels, president of the Waverly Group, and she'll tell you why she insists on red rooms. "Energy, passion, love of life—when you project that, you get it back," she says. Talk to British decorator Nina Campbell, and she'll confess, "You should always have a red chair, because it makes shy people feel better." Visit Texan Carol Bolton, the queen of casual, and she'll admit, "It takes work to make something look this undecorated."

Decorating, contrary to popular opinion, isn't easy. It takes work—the hard work of knowing what *you* love. Join us for a journey to see just how fulfilling making a home can be.

Family Style

❧

Home, a word that hums with familiar, warm emotion. *Decorating*, a word that evokes perfection and order. *Family style*, a marriage of the chic and the comfortable, the beautiful and the truly livable.

LIVABILITY FIRST

Rachel Ashwell

- ✍ *Founder of the trendsetting Shabby Chic stores and author of style books.*

- ✍ *Home base: A rented house on the beach in Malibu, California.*

- ✍ *Style signature: Spruced-up flea-market finds.*

- ✍ *Decorating requirements: With two children and lots of sandy feet, she insists on "quality that you don't have to be neurotic about."*

White canvas shades drawn up, Rachel Ashwell's windows open on the ever-changing blue of the Pacific Ocean. "My days are so cluttered with stuff, I love looking out and having nothing in front of me," she says.

One of home furnishing's great innovators, Rachel opened the first Shabby Chic store in 1989 in Santa Monica, California. Divorced and with two small children, she translated her personal look—baggy slipcovers over flea-market furniture, mirrors with chips and charm, funky lamps with stylish shades—into a shop. Success came fast and furious, and it quickly depleted her stock, so Rachel found herself with a

second career—reproducing favorite pieces and designing new ones.

Her home remains her laboratory. Though she is always re-decorating, she sticks to hard-and-fast rules: "I never buy anything unless I have a use for it—no tchotchkes." She insists on versatility—a dining chair as a piano bench, a cake plate to hold bathroom soaps. And she never strays from her color scheme—tones as pale as the inside of a seashell—even if it means buying a white piano for her children. "Half of me felt it was very flashy and Liberace-ish," she confesses, "but now I like it."

Still, Rachel is a holdout for old-fashioned elegance. "It's so easy to say, 'Oh, it doesn't matter, just get out the paper plates,'" she explains. "Pretty soon your whole life becomes 'It doesn't matter.'" She believes in silver and crystal for dinner, even if dinner is hot dogs. But her linen napkins are unironed, the silver mismatched. If a floral plate breaks, she just shrugs—it cost a song at a flea market, and surely she'll find another.

Using mirrors, opposite, Rachel enhances her expansive views, page 15. A huge mirror edged in fleur-de-lis molding is reflected by another mirror over the fireplace. For chair slipcovers, above, and pillows, Rachel uses a mix of vintage fabrics. Sometimes she'll wash chintz in hot water to dull its sheen, or add a bit of bleach to fade it. She relies on black tea mixed into a tub of water when whites need to be aged.

Most of what Rachel owns has a flea-market pedigree, but things rarely come home "as is." For her living room, she dressed up a round table with hardware-store molding, and a mercury-glass lamp got a new shade. Little side tables, cleaned of peeling paint, were chosen "because they're just the right height to stretch your arm out and put down a drink." The sisal rug obscures the broadloom carpeting that came with her rental. "When we move, we'll find half the beach underneath," she says.

In the living room, she holds fast to her aesthetic, insisting on

a grown-up expanse of white, made practical with washable slip-

covers. She likes put-your-feet-up coffee tables and considers round

to be the most hospitable shape, since it draws guests into a circle.

What's on the side tables? Accessories, such as they are, tend to be

books that are actually read and seashells gathered by the children.

Though Rachel considers the whole house to be a refuge,

she regards her bedroom as her sanctuary. Her bed is copied from

one she found in a flea market, and the linens are adapted from

vintage designs—all examples of her personal vision. "One of the

lovely things about decorating from flea markets," she says, "is that

no one is dictating to you. When your house reflects your own

choices, it affects your life in a fundamental way."

Rachel's bedroom, opposite and above, contains just the essentials: a chest of drawers, a whitewashed bed patterned after an antique (she avoids old beds because of the potential hazards of lead paint and the problem of nonstandard sizes), a glass-knobbed nightstand, also copied, and a generous chaise longue. "It's wonderful to read here at night," Rachel says. "When my children have nightmares, they come here and sleep."

NEVER ENOUGH RED

Katrin Cargill

ᴓᴘ Decorator, magazine editor, and author of a series of stylish how-to books.

ᴓᴘ Home base: London.

ᴓᴘ Style signature: Red and white, white and red—a two-color scheme that gives her rooms focus and infinite variety.

ᴓᴘ Visual inspiration: Switzerland, her mother's homeland, where "red gingham curtains hang in nearly every cottage window."

Some people collect Staffordshire or coin silver. Katrin Cargill collects reds, whether in shoes, sweaters, eyeglasses, or striped cushions. Extra fabrics in reds fill the storage bin in her living room's checked ottoman. "The attic never needs insulating— I have so many slipcovers up there," she says, laughing.

But Katrin is choosy about her reds. She avoids fire-engine and sports-car hues, concentrating instead on the faded pinks of vintage textiles. "It all goes back to my childhood in the Alps," says Katrin, who was raised on red-and-white towels and bed linens. "I keep thinking this is a phase, but it hasn't passed."

Decorating with two colors requires a sure hand. "You have to use sparks of complementary color," explains Katrin, who set yellow daffodils on her desk, trimmed windows with sky blue, and painted a love seat apple green. "But you want surprises, unpredictability,

"With red and white, you can mix any number of styles and everything looks great."

too," so she introduced touches of black as well: the legs of a wing chair, two striped taffeta lampshades, the frames for a suite of prints above the sofa. Black, she points out, is a foil for the red and white, and it keeps the room from looking like a Valentine.

Katrin's passion for red is taken in stride by her husband, David, and son, Harrison, who indulge her with gifts of ladybug stationery and checked teacups. "They find red things wherever we go," Katrin says with a laugh. But she's careful not to let her red treasures take over. She may hang a heart from a drawer pull or stack

Eighteenth-century prints, opposite, are framed in black to balance the red in the living room. The prints, which hang across from the fireplace, page 23, go right up to the ceiling, a trick that makes a small room look more majestic. The strict grid of the arrangement and the geometric checks on the sofa are softened with flounces on the slipcover skirt and the lampshade. The oversize pillows on the sofa are reversible.

25

Though the distance from the dining table to the bay window, right, is short, the room seems more spacious because of its disciplined color scheme. Katrin makes the most of the space she has by drawing the eye upward: Instead of long curtains, there are Roman shades pulled high; small pictures top large ones, like the tiny photo of her son hung above a framed coronation scarf. Several blue boxes, above, add what Katrin calls a color surprise, which helps take the edge off so much red.

red and white boxes on her desk, but she doesn't want anything brazen enough to upstage the decorating focal point of the house.

To make sure that her red-and-white fabrics take center stage, she's careful to keep the background neutral. Walls are ivory, the rug sea-grass. "When you're using red and white—the classic homespun pattern—you don't want a lot of fuss and frills."

What keeps Katrin's style fresh is the range of historical references she incorporates. She gravitates toward Gustavian checks, which are used throughout the living room, but she also includes a reproduction French document print, a Provençal pillow, an American house portrait, and a framed 1902 British coronation scarf. "Visiting Sweden made me brave enough to go with a very simple scheme," says Katrin, who came home determined to pare down the cozy clutter typical of English style. But she's not cut out to be a true minimalist: The drape of a table skirt and the flounce of a lampshade are just too seductive for a textile collector to resist.

An apple-green bench tucked behind the living room's round table, opposite, serves as a quiet nook for breakfast. Its curving lines are loosely repeated in the flange of the checked pillow. In little red still lifes of napkins, china, berries, stationery, and flowers, above and opposite, Katrin experiments with all sorts of combinations of red.

SHADES OF SOPHISTICATION

"Once you start looking at people's lamps and what they put on them, you quickly realize the lampshade is one of the last things to be considered in a room," writes Katrin Cargill in her how-to book *Lampshades*. The mood of a room can be "instantly changed by the addition of the right lampshade, the right light, and the right amount of it."

She recommends rethinking the silhouette of the lamp as a whole. Rather than the typical Empire, or conical, shade, perhaps a triangle or square or something as silly as an old aunt's hat would be just the thing. To make a shade, ribbons can be woven, silk can be pleated, or voile shirred. Keep in mind that "the type of material you choose will affect the quality of light shed by the shade. Whites and light solids radiate the most light."

One easy way to alter a lamp's look is to "slipcover" an existing shade, as Katrin did, opposite, by adding a shirred fabric skirt—here made from a vintage tea towel. She has used the same technique to turn voile into a wisp of a tutu. She has even designed apricot linen sconce slipcovers that are like 1950s circle skirts, flaring gracefully on the bias. "Shade slipcovers are wonderful," Katrin says. "Whenever you rearrange your furniture or make a change in your decorating, you can update the look of your lamps."

Lyn Peterson

🎵 *Decorator, textile designer, and owner of Motif Designs, a fabric and wallpaper company.*

🎵 *Home base: a 1927 Colonial-Revival house in Westchester County, New York.*

🎵 *Style signature: Mixing her grandmother's needlepoint and her mother's silver with a parade of children and dogs.*

🎵 *Life lesson: "Years ago, I had a canvas sofa. Then I had a dog. And then I had a child. I got rid of the natural canvas sofa."*

Though she's a textile designer and decorator, Lyn Peterson had much less to say about the look of her 1920s Colonial-style house than did her grandmother, her great-aunt Hilma, and a long list of long-deceased relatives. "I came with a lot of decorating baggage," says Lyn, who inherited everything from a grand piano to bamboo porch furniture. "I didn't get to steer my own course." Dismayed by what she sees as our disposable decorating society, she was ready to rise to the challenge of creating a home out of hand-me-downs.

Knowing that she would never have thirty guests for dinner, she took a section from her grandmother's long dining

table and cut down its pedestal to make a coffee table. She mounted

her relatives' eyeglasses on velvet, commemorating each owner with

a tiny brass plaque. And she gave wing chairs, ottomans, and arm-

chairs her own imprint, reupholstering them in fabrics that flow

from room to room in shades of sage and olive, claret and terra-cotta.

"I like to think of rooms as a community," says Lyn, who set

her stream of colors against a neutral backdrop: a whitewashed

wood floor and beige walls in the living room, beige raw-silk

curtains throughout. "Window treatments are a huge investment.

Labor is expensive even if the fabric isn't," she explains. "I always do

neutrals so that my curtains will last the life of the house."

At heart, however, she's in love with pattern. But she believes

in using prints on either furniture or walls, never both. In the living

room, a burst of color comes from the floral on the sofas. "It's

impervious to grape juice and ink," says Lyn, who has a child in

grammar school, another in graduate school, and two in between.

Between sets of beige-curtained French doors in the living room, opposite, Lyn added light with a mirrored panel. In the dining room, above, she included armchairs for a more relaxed look and turned a pine dresser into a practical sideboard by setting a piece of marble on top. A screened porch, page 33, carries the same casual yet traditional sensibility to the outside of the house.

In the dining room, where the furniture is "wood, wood, wood—a forest of legs," she papered the walls with a paisley that echoes her grandmother's Oriental rug. "I like intimate dining rooms," she maintains, explaining that enveloping patterns create a

"Life is high-maintenance enough. I look at white linen and think, No, not for me."

cozy feeling, even in large rooms. For intimacy, her chandelier and wall sconces are on dimmers to mimic the flicker of candlelight.

One of the few areas in which Lyn was able to chart new territory was accessories. She believes in displaying what you love, and in her case that includes her collection of antique finials, arrayed on living room tables and shelves, her husband's childhood stamp collection, and her children's art. "We can all go out and buy the same things," she says. "A house isn't interesting unless it reflects the people who live there."

A folding leather screen, opposite, that once belonged to Lyn's great-aunt now hides a vent and softens a living room corner. Its pattern is echoed in the serpentine swirls of the upholstery on the Louis XV-style bergère, also an inherited piece. For extra seating, a radiator becomes a window banquette.

Adjoining Lyn's pale bedroom is an old-fashioned sleeping porch, right, that she painted dark green for "an exclamation point." On warm nights, she says, "the porch is so popular that the children practically stand in line for tickets." An old pine cabinet, above, is devoted to children's toys, art, and summer treasures from the seashore.

CREATING CHILDPROOF STYLE

As a mother of four, Lyn Peterson has no patience with a velvet-rope decorating policy. "There's an insane level of activity at our house," she says, explaining that she usually has "eleven ten-year-olds screaming through." Her living room's whitewashed floor has survived roller skates, the dining room's Oriental rug has elegantly camouflaged spills, and antiques like the Scandinavian bench, opposite, have already accommodated generations of wear. Every room of Lyn's house can be lived in, thanks to a firm set of decorating rules.

The carpet should match the dog's fur or whatever else the household doles out. Her carpet is beige ("the color of dust") and made of wool ("synthetics stain; a nail brush and soapy water will clean most spots on wool").

Children, of course, come with dirt *and* toys. "I just organize the toys," says Lyn. "I'm big on baskets." In the kitchen, she designates drawers for toys; in the family room, cabinets below the TV. And what about all the projects toted home from school? "I keep every piece of art, every silly thread thing," says Lyn. She's appointed an antique pine cupboard as a shrine to her children's creations and hung an ever-changing gallery in the downstairs bathroom. She designs around her children, just as she designs around her great-great-grandfather, who painted the landscape, opposite.

Interiors as Art

❧

Their homes are their canvases, backdrops designed to

satisfy a penchant for line, texture, and color. Whether

the furnishings are new or antique, ready-made or

hand-crafted, every corner is a careful composition.

Carolyn Quartermaine

⚬ Painter turned designer—of fabrics, interiors, parties, even Japanese department-store windows.

⚬ Home base: A large, open-plan flat in London.

⚬ Style signature: Her fabrics and interiors always look one-of-a-kind.

⚬ Inspiration: "Japanese art. I love the way it's very fine, very soft and delicate. The Japanese can say a lot with just one brush stroke."

"I try to keep my flat very peaceful. I need a very blank canvas all the time," says Carolyn Quartermaine, who lives and paints in a loftlike London apartment. Her furnishings are an assortment of deliberately spare vintage chairs, 1950s folding art tables—one she cut down to make a coffee table, another she brings out for dinner parties—and impromptu curtains made by draping fabrics over poles.

But such conscious paring down belies Carolyn's love of intense color and antiques of all sorts. "I take pieces in and out of storage," she says, "or someone will ask me to decorate an apartment in Rome, and suddenly fifteen pieces go off to a

client." When decorating her own home, Carolyn's usual method is to upholster antique furniture with white canvas and pin on fabrics she brings home from her silk-screen studio. Her tablecloth and napkins, all unhemmed, might display swirls, flowers, or richly lettered prints. "Whatever I'm working on in the studio becomes the look of the moment," she says.

Despite such artistic flux, there are constants. Her furniture always has fine lines. "There is a specific style I like," she explains. "It might be 1960s or 1920s, but it always has a certain delicacy." Perched on her radiators are two seventeenth-century English gates with serpentine grilles and flowers that remind her of embroidery.

She particularly loves furniture that's gilded, especially if the gleam has worn away over time to reveal an undercoat of white gesso. On her fabrics, she often applies gold paint. "Gold is both a wonderful color and an embellishment," she says. "It makes fabrics—or furniture—very, very rich."

Carolyn's flat is designed for change. The cushions of her Louis XV-style sofa, page 45, are reversible. Her dining table, opposite and above, is a folding art table that can be put away after parties. Here it is draped in the project of the moment, silk-screened swirls.

"When I come back from Japan, I have fans and packages all over the flat for weeks," says Carolyn. "Then I pare down." She also likes to bring home her one-of-a-kind fabrics, tacking them to a chair, opposite, to change her look instantly. Even her art—filigreed gates and a couture dress, above—is casually placed. "I rarely have things made up for my home," she says.

No matter what phase she is in, Carolyn's walls are always white and her accent colors are consistently clear. "I don't like beige," she maintains. "It's dirty." Instead, she relies on accents of pale lilacs, faint greens, barely-there yellows, and gentle grays—colors that appear naturally as the sunlight shifts and the walls take on reflections from fabrics and furnishings.

Among these clear neutrals, Carolyn is especially fond of gray, the color of the eau-de-Nil silk taffeta on her sofa. "Gray is a classic," she says. "If you look at French châteaus or historic Swedish houses, you always see gray. It's wonderful with white, and almost any color looks good against it."

Carolyn's blank-canvas theory of decorating means that her flat is usually bare of art, unless you count an Alexander McQueen dress she acquired when she was working for Givenchy. "I can get into it, but I don't wear it," she says of the virtually transparent garment. "I love it for the flowers and the brushwork."

To Carolyn, that brushwork is key. She is a master at experimenting with the effect of paint on fabric. "My work is very much about making marks," she says. "I'm very inspired by Japanese art and the way so much is said with a single brush stroke." The Japanese, conversely, are inspired by Carolyn: A major department store asked her to design its windows. She returns from her frequent trips to Tokyo armed with trinkets—fans and sweets chosen for their exquisite packaging—which she sets out as if they were prized art.

"I love the way the Japanese pay attention to everyday beauty," Carolyn says. "To me it's the little things that count—really good coffee in a white cup, a jar of jam and a rose on your breakfast table. I love to take unexpected objects and give them importance. Sometimes I'll put Indian bracelets in a silver dish on a table or repot a foxglove in a paint pot. You don't need porcelain and cut crystal, but you must have something the eye can marvel over." On every level, Carolyn's pared-down apartment is designed to do just that.

Carolyn hasn't found the right bed—hence the mattress on the floor, opposite—but she has found the right headboard: a gilded one from eighteenth-century Venice. The eiderdown was her grandmother's, the walls are buff plaster, and the Florentine-inspired fabric is hung over a pole as a sort of door. Pinned right to the wall, above, she keeps snippets of the colors and patterns that infuse her current work.

SPECIALIZING IN SUNSHINE

Isabelle de Borchgrave

- *Artist and designer of everything from fabrics to framed prints, cards to rugs, all displayed at her Brussels, Belgium, shop.*

- *Home base: A town house in Brussels.*

- *Style signature: Rich colors that banish the gray of city life.*

- *Ace up her sleeve: Her paintbrush, which she uses to decorate one-of-a-kind fabrics.*

- *Design philosophy: "I don't like things to look new. I prefer when you see the life span."*

Isabelle de Borchgrave loves light—a certain kind of sun-drenched Mediterranean light that is scarce in Brussels. But no matter that she lives in a northern clime. Isabelle does her best to banish the city's natural pallor with a bold wall of yellow taffeta in her bedroom and rich colors throughout the house. "Red and black and green are hot colors—you need them in Belgium," she says.

In addition to deep colors, Isabelle uses fabric to promote warmth and intimacy, draping tables and adding canopies to beds. She lowered the height of an architectural beam in her bedroom with a zigzag valance, visually dividing the room

into two parts, one for sleeping, the other for work. "I have an art studio a block away, but I like to keep a table here in case I get an idea in the middle of the night," she explains.

Sitting beneath her candlelit chandelier, which she says is so nice in winter, Isabelle dreams up patterns like those for the richly colored rugs that are part of her ready-made oeuvre. Mostly, though, when she designs for her own home, she paints one-of-a-kind fabrics, including the strip of Persian tendrils that intersects her billowing yellow curtains. "By painting, I get to know how fabric works," she says. She has even gone so far as to replicate historical costumes—flowing period gowns complete with tucks, ruffles, and bustles—using only paint and paper.

By plying her brush rather than seeking out factory-made prints, Isabelle is able to scale patterns to suit furniture, place floral designs just so, and avoid repeats. "Paint gives more life," she explains. "When people come to my house, they immediately want

In her library, opposite, Isabelle's art extends from framed fruit prints that flank the fireplace mirror to the painted fabric on the vintage fauteuil. "After twelve years the fabric is very nice," she says, approving of the effects of time and wear. On the library bookshelves, she layers mirrors and paintings over books, creating eye-catching vignettes. The collage, above, was made by a friend, but the writing instruments are hers: "I love nice pens. When I travel I am always painting or drawing."

Isabelle positioned a sofa and chairs around a beautifully carved table, opposite. "In winter we have dinner parties here," she says. By using the library's two round tables, she can seat eighteen. In the dining room, which overlooks the garden, Isabelle painted frames, above, for three large mirrors, borrowing patterns from her collection of blue-and-white delftware.

to touch the chairs." That goes for the pillows, too, which she painted to appear as tapestry and needlepoint. "I like to play with trompe l'oeil," she says.

Always, though, light is at the heart of Isabelle's decorating, even in the library, a windowless room set between the sitting room, with its street-side views, and the dining room, which is adjacent to the garden. Here she relies on intimate pools of lamplight, reflected by the white moiré on the walls. Above the fireplace, she added a light-catching mirror, using an antique door molding for the frame. More mirrors filling in for clear panes of glass on the tall doors add to the room's gleam and sparkle, but Isabelle doesn't take credit for their presence. "Before we moved in, the house was a dance studio," she explains. Nonetheless, she loves the doors, explaining that "every time you move them, you discover another view." And another reflection of her soul-warming palette.

For daughter Pauline's bedroom, right, Isabelle created a Turkish fantasy, draping a canopy over suspended poles. The wallpapers—two prints and two borders—illustrate her interest in stenciling. They are her own designs, as are the framed prints and the bed fabrics. The gold flowers on the Turkish scallops are hand painted, just the right flourish to finish the bed. A huge age-spotted mirror, above, leans against the wall in Isabelle's bedroom; the tiny bags were made by Pauline.

A PASSION
FOR COLOR

Anna French

- *Textile designer with a London shop and to-the-trade showrooms in New York and Boston.*

- *Home base: A double-fronted nineteenth-century London house.*

- *Bon mot: "I couldn't live without color—after all, I went to art school in the sixties, which were all about pattern and color."*

Though she was born and bred beneath the gray skies of England, Anna French lives for color. And not the tweedy range one might expect but, rather, the kind of hothouse pinks and oranges that burst from flower markets.

"Actually, going to a flower shop is a great way to learn about color," says Anna, who recommends putting together a bouquet on the spot. "Pick up two flowers—maybe a purple tulip and an orange gerbera daisy. Add a third color, and a fourth. Then put one back. You need to experiment."

Anna continues the experiment at home. "In a flower shop, masses of color look great," she explains, "but if you take

a bouquet home and dot the flowers about a room, the intensity

is lost. Color needs to be grouped."

At first glance, the rooms in her own home look more like

color saturations than groupings, yet they are conceived with lots of

room to breathe. In her living room, for example, the floor is stone

tile, so the furniture appears to float on a neutral sea. One wall is a

ragged and stippled combination of greens, yellow, and turquoise;

the three surrounding walls are unadulterated white.

In daughter Amy's bedroom, a Mediterranean blue vibrates

from the wallpaper to the windows, but the strength of the hue is

balanced by bare wood floorboards and a skirtless iron bed that

is intended to show them off.

Anna describes Amy's sprigged wallpaper—blue with under-

tones of pink that warm the room's northern exposure—as plain.

Yet the paper's background, composed of numerous shades of

blue, is lively. Anna is a great believer in using a range of tones.

In an entry, page 61, Anna displays one
of her watercolor collections. Once inside
the main part of her house, all is bold and
bright. In the living room, opposite, the
wall is textured with five shades of green
acrylic paint and finished with a coat of
varnish, the work of an artist friend.
The curtain, above, has panels of pattern,
revealed when the folds are loosened.

To warm up the blue in her daughter's room, above and opposite, Anna added healthy helpings of pink in the pillow shams and duvet cover. Some of the iron bed's old black paint was rubbed off to show the gray metal underneath; the exposed metal was then varnished for rust protection. The armoire, a fitting from Anna's shop, is curtained with the same print used on Amy's windows.

One example she often uses to illustrate her point: "Grass is never just one shade of green."

Neither is her living room. On clean-lined upholstery, pillows, and painted armoires, she used five distinct greens. "If you mix only two, they might clash, but if you mix half a dozen and keep to clear, bright tones, you replicate nature," she explains.

And what about pattern? "You can only have one intense pattern in a room," Anna says firmly. "If you go for nice, bright, colorful curtains"—like those at Amy's window—"you want to be sure nothing in the rest of the room fights it. You want to keep things simple. To me, Amy's wallpaper is simple. The mottled green wall in the living room is simple."

Private Sanctuaries

Where to nest with the proverbial cup of tea? In a converted barn, a garden pavilion, a well-pillowed corner. Anywhere will do if the colors soothe and the environment is designed to nurture the soul.

RULES FOR A REFUGE

Lillian August

- *Textile and furniture designer, and owner—with her three sons—of three Lillian August shops in Connecticut.*

- *Home base: Palm Beach County, Florida, and Westport, Connecticut.*

- *Style signature: English country comfort scaled to American taste.*

- *Emotional leitmotif: Colors that re-create the amber glow of firelight and candlelight.*

Lillian August likes to talk about decorating in terms of nurturing, as in "the shelter of a nurturing sofa" or fabrics that reflect "the nurturing color of firelight." She believes that a room should tell a story, and her narrative hinges on what she considers to be the cornerstone of a room: the sofa. "If it exudes comfort, so will the rest of the room," she says. She points out that because it's almost always the largest piece of furniture in a room, a sofa should be selected before paint and fabrics are chosen. Its style, shape, and upholstery—Edwardian or 1920s, thick arm or thin, exposed legs or skirt—will, more than any other piece, determine a room's mood.

Lillian believes in sofas that are long—at least eighty-nine inches, even in a small room—and deep enough to curl up in, "though you do want your feet to touch the floor when you're sitting up." Backs can be tufted or composed of throw pillows, but the finished piece must convey a feeling of comfort.

To create that feeling, Lillian employs a few tricks. First, she washes fabrics before upholstering. "They acquire a wonderful hand and a vintage feel," she says. In addition, she understuffs the cushions, using more down than foam, so the sofa doesn't have the plump newness that is so typical of department-store purchases. "I love English country homes where pieces have been handed down for generations," she explains.

She makes sure her rooms have an illusion of inherited character by choosing disparate armchairs—here one is leather, another tufted, with little castors on its front legs. Her side tables are a mix of shapes and woods, and her coffee table is large enough to hold a

Unlike some decorators, Lillian believes in placing the sofa directly in front of the fireplace, above, relying on its symbolism to create emotional warmth. Here the sofa and armchairs, opposite and page 69—all her designs—have the turned legs and fine detailing of Victorian and Edwardian pieces. The seating area is anchored by a large patterned rug, creating a sense of intimacy within a spacious room.

A tufted piano bench, above, doubles as a side table; its lid opens for storage. Lillian likes to accessorize with hats, walking sticks, and items that are often forgotten in closets. In a seating nook, opposite, the tailored crispness of checks contrasts with pretty dressmaker pillows. "It's typically English to go from the feminine to the masculine," she says.

family's current books or pastimes and sturdy enough to support the inevitable feet. And just as textures are mixed—leather and chenille, needlepoint and polished wood—so are furniture pedigrees.

For colors, Lillian relies on sunlit golds, Renaissance reds, and bookbinding greens because of the way they combine to create "a cloistered, insular feeling." But before she looks at a paint chip or picks up a fabric swatch, she decides on a rug, because "it's a room's pattern focal point." Last on her list of decorating decisions: curtain fabric, which never steals the show. In the living room, the curtains are made of the same textured weave that covers the tufted arm-chair. But often she leaves windows entirely bare. In the world according to Lillian August, the focal point of a room should be where the people are—curled up in front of the fireplace.

- *Designer and proprietor of five shops in Fredericksburg, Texas, including Homestead, Idle Hours, and Bolton & Bolton.*

- *Home base: A turn-of-the-century farm set on eighty acres of maize and milo, oak and thistle.*

- *Style signature: Looks-as-if-it's-always-been-there chic.*

- *Bon mot: "It takes work to make something look this undecorated."*

- *Creative process: A good pot of coffee, a nightgown, a pencil, a clean table, and a stolen hour.*

HOMESPUN ELEGANCE

Carol Bolton

"If I were decorating for you," says Carol Bolton, "I'd have you get out all the things you love. Not the things someone gave you or the things that are expensive. Just what you really and truly love. Then I'd come up with six or ten colors, and we'd do the whole house."

Some people start with furniture, some people start with pattern, but Carol designs almost entirely by color. When she decided it was time to decorate her barn, she walked right outside and gathered stalks of grasses and wildflowers in sage greens, faded yellows, ripened apricot, and dusty reds—the look of the Texas landscape in summer. Snippings in hand,

she set about gathering talismans with the same hues: an old glove case, glasses, swatches, and trims. These were not necessarily intended as part of the finished room; the process is simply Carol's way of getting to know her palette. The defining moment came when she found a piece of fabric that captured all of her colors in its swirls. She used it on the sofa pillows and the coverlet in the barn's loft. "I carried it around in my pocket for weeks," she says.

But a color scheme alone isn't enough for Carol. She also needs a narrative, a story of the past told through coffee tables and lighting fixtures. For this interior, she penned a tale about antiques being brought down from the rafters—even though the barn's darkest corners yielded little more than rusty nails—and accessories acquired over generations. It is a homespun American version of the style mix long admired in English country houses.

To bring her narrative to life, Carol assembled straight-back chairs with horsehair peeking out from worn leather seats and odd

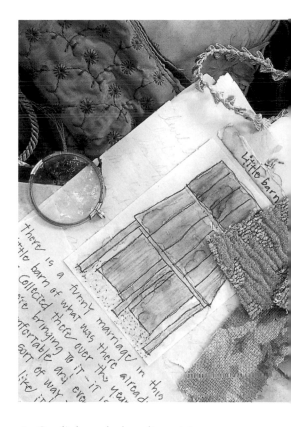

In Carol's barn, dyed muslin curtains, opposite, are hung on handmade rings of bailing wire. The curtains are yards longer than the window, but Carol tucks the excess on the sill, imagining that they were found in the attic. Before she began decorating, she gathered examples of her palette—an old glove case, olive-rimmed glasses, swatches and trims, above—as a way of getting to know her color possibilities.

lamp parts to wire together into chandeliers. These she mixed with new furnishings—a sofa, an arm chair, and an ottoman, all her own designs. In Carol's hands, these pieces look decades old. The ottoman is covered in velvet, dyed to suggest an ancient patina. The rest of the upholstery is a patchwork of prints and trims.

"When you have a store and access to wonderful things,
at some point you want to stop decorating and start living."

On the side of her barn, page 75, Carol added a sleeping porch composed of old screen doors, all found by her builder on the side of the road. Four doors constitute a permanent wall, while another four open, French-door style. An army cot plumped with a new handmade mattress, opposite, accommodates naps; side chairs can travel out to the garden. The floor is a crazy quilt of local stone.

"I wanted it to look as if a new cushion or skirt had been added over the years," she explains. In the loft and on the sleeping porch, she stitched the edges of new cotton mattresses to give them a rumpled look, and she covered an old chest by attaching velvet with fabric glue, deliberately leaving the frayed edges showing. "I collect things that have been repaired," says Carol. "I just love the way someone will fix a wood bowl by appliquéing a piece of tin, secured with tiny nails. Imperfections add mystery."

Carol also gave small works of art a similar storied past. She hung a scissored picture in an old purse clasp, looping a trailing thread around the tail of a glued-on dog. "I imagined the girl holding the dog in her arms," she explains. For pressed flowers, Carol chose the most casual presentation. She mounted blossoms on velvet or aged paper and framed them with cardboard and glass, edged with tape. Sometimes the tape is dyed, sometimes it's decorated with a bit of velvet ribbon or braid, but that's as fancy as Carol gets. "New frames," she maintains, "are too pretty for me."

Pictures are hung so that she can rearrange them easily. Pressed flowers are slipped behind bailing wire; other flea-market frames dangle on dyed twine from a nail or a doorknob. "I like rooms to look casual, as if they just happened," Carol explains. Though that takes time, "it's worth it when you have a simple environment, beautifully colored, filled with your favorite things."

Carol stained the walls of the barn with "this funny green paint" that "looks totally original." It is visible behind her framed flowers and in the sleeping loft, opposite top and bottom. There the bed has a princess-and-the-pea appearance, thanks to an excess of featherbeds and pillows. Pinned to the oversize tufted headboard is an old photograph, above, framed in a salvaged purse clasp.

ACQUIRING AGE

Were the sturdy German immigrants who built this barn to return, they would find a world faded to sepia, for Carol has banished every hint of white. She darkened curtain scrim—torn, and hung on bailing wire—to an olivey gold by bathing it in her own mixture of Rit dye. She mottled a golden velvet, destined for a new ottoman, with a similar mossy mixture, deepened by the addition of a cup of coffee. "I do a variation on tie-dyeing," Carol says. "I bunch up the fabric, throw it in, and bunch it up and dye it again so that I get lots of variations of color."

Ticking for bed pillows and mattresses is dipped in tea to take off the edge. Even an old map of Fredericksburg, Texas, was too bright for Carol's taste—she aged it by blotting on dye with a dry brush. "Sometimes there are things you want to use but they're just too clean," she says with a sigh. "But you can take a clipping from today's newspaper and bake it in a toaster oven to give it a sixty-year-old glow."

Another aging technique: Carol creates light fixtures from odd parts and fits out bare bulbs with homemade wire shades, covered in coffee-dipped scrim. To suspend her fixtures, she uses fabric-covered automotive wire found in junk stores. "It has the most beautiful shade of gold with red flecks in it," says Carol, who loves to find beauty in forgotten places.

≈ *Magazine editor, product designer, and author of style books.*

≈ *Home base: An 1874 brownstone in New York City and an 1846 cottage in Yaphank, Long Island.*

≈ *Style signature: Natural colors, vintage linens, classical simplicity.*

≈ *Current fascination: Colonial Williamsburg, "for the way it combines architectural richness and a spare decorative aesthetic."*

CULTIVATING OUTDOOR SPACES

Tricia Foley

Someone's always camping out at Tricia Foley's—her twin nephews, a photographer on assignment, a friend from England. But Tricia's tiny bay-and-a-half Cape on historic Main Street in Yaphank, Long Island, has just one bedroom. Reluctant to plan an addition that would alter the character of the house, Tricia decided to get more space the old-fashioned way: by building a garden pavilion-cum-guest room as well as a porch, hidden behind the front of the house, that serves as a summer dining room.

An avid researcher, Tricia has always loved the outbuildings at Colonial Williamsburg. "I'd come home with roll after

roll of pictures," she says. She delved into the records of Yaphank's historical society and discovered that her house once had a summer kitchen. "You could see the lines of the foundation in the grass," she says. Tricia plotted her garden cottage to be roughly the same size—ten feet deep and sixteen feet wide. It sits at the end of the yard on a cinderblock foundation, which, when excavated, yielded domestic evidence of the nineteenth century. "We found lots of bits of Staffordshire and creamware," says Tricia, who, coincidentally, collects both.

Fitted with French doors and white canvas curtains, the garden cottage has acquired a following far and wide. Tricia's nieces and nephews beg for a chance to sleep over, and friends call ahead for reservations. Part of the cottage's appeal is its playhouse scale and its lack of contemporary amenities. At night, guests venture from the main house carrying a lantern; they read by candlelight and sleep beneath a canopy of mosquito netting.

Tricia designed the garden pavilion, page 85, with cedar shingles and beige paint so that it would look like a replica of the house. Guests sleeping on the banquette, opposite, rely on candlelight and mosquito netting, here tied in a knot to pull it aside. On the porch of the house, above, the table and chairs stay out year-round. "I used to entertain on the lawn," Tricia says, "but I had to move all the furniture every time I mowed."

The living area is bookended by closets—little rooms in themselves—that provide storage. One houses garden supplies, the other boxes of books, files, and Christmas ornaments.

With her guest cottage finished, Tricia was ready for a porch. For years she'd wanted a proper outdoor eating area. Finally she settled on a simple design—stock railing and posts, pressure-treated lumber, and the standing-seam metal roofing often used on barns. "I wanted a porch that looks like it's always been there," she says.

Invisible from Main Street, the porch occupies the indent created by the house's ell. It shades the kitchen, shields the side door from rain and snow, and provides space for a table, chairs, and a cupboard full of plates and bowls. "Now I light the citronella candles, and I'm ready to entertain."

Convenience aside, Tricia's satisfaction with the porch is its simplicity. "When you have a house with historic value, you have to keep its character in mind when you make changes."

"I love gardening," says Tricia, "but I never had a place for it. The potting soil was under the kitchen sink, the trowels by the back stoop." Now Tricia keeps her supplies in the closets, above and opposite, in her new garden house: clay pots, a watering can, and secateurs— and picnic supplies—all have a place.

A Garden House in a Weekend

Much like an Amish barn raising, the construction of Tricia Foley's garden house—a ten-by-eight-foot room flanked by two three-foot-deep closets—happened in a weekend. "My brothers came over and my father was there giving advice. It was a free-for-all," Tricia says. Aside from her good-natured labor pool, the secret to such a speedy building project was careful planning and the use of readily available materials. The walls are standard eight-foot plywood; French doors and moldings are all stock. Bead board, less expensive than wainscoting, lines the interior. The only nonstandard items: a pair of vintage half-round windows that illuminate the closets.

Inside, Tricia's furniture consists of a ten-foot banquette that serves as both a guest bed ("my nephews sleep end to end") and a storage unit. Underneath the mattress—a piece of foam rubber wrapped in Dacron Poly-fil and upholstered with beige ticking—there is room to stow garden umbrellas and folding lawn chairs. Tricia painted the floor with khaki-colored deck paint. "I wanted to be able to sweep it out or hose it down," she says.

Though the garden house is surprisingly warm in winter—its French doors face south; the north side has no windows—cold-weather sleepover guests are few. But Tricia visits often, with a cup of tea and a shawl.

Laboratories of White

Cockleshells, lilies of the valley, sheets drying in the sun. There are as many shades of white as there are clouds in the sky. So those who love decorating with white are always dipping a brush in a new can of paint.

CHANGING WITH THE SEASONS

Mary Baltz

ℐ *Decorator and editor.*

ℐ *Home base: Southampton, New York.*

ℐ *Style signature: White, white, and more white.*

ℐ *Bravest move: Taking a brush to her grandmother's mahogany table, which has seen eight different coats of white since she inherited it.*

What colors an all-white interior, as Mary Baltz knows well, is light. The same furniture, the same crystal, take on an entirely different character depending on whether they are flooded by the summer's high sun or warmed by the yellow glow of a winter afternoon.

As the seasons change, Mary's rooms change with them. In early summer, she performs the traditional task of rolling up rugs ("I want to be able to broom-sweep the sand") and lightening her look—taking down a valance or two, moving an armchair out to the porch, bringing wicker into the living room. In winter, her pillows are a warm mix of tartan and

needlepoint; in summer, she relies strictly on lace and matelassé. "I'm always going up and down to the attic," she says with a laugh.

To make room for her extensive collection of vintage pillow shams, Mary replaced the manufacturer's cushions on the back of her sofa with a series of square European bed pillows that she can dress and re-dress to her heart's content. She considers all of these changeable elements to be the house's wardrobe.

Essential to any wardrobe are accessories, and these Mary also arranges with a careful eye to the season. In summer she sets empty white frames on the coffee table and brings out her collections of white hats and seashells, silver and crystal—"I mix my grandmother's cut glass with Waterford from my wedding." In winter she makes a cozier setting with piles of books and cashmere throws. She returns the crystal to the cupboards but keeps the silver on display, letting it tarnish so it will softly reflect candlelight. "I love dull silver in winter," she says. "It has such comforting effect."

In a white room, accessories need to be simple. On a white coffee table, page 95, Mary sets out empty white frames, sometimes using them to showcase her daughter's art. By the window, opposite, she gives silver and crystal a light-catching setting on her grandmother's table. Porch furniture, above, prevails indoors and out.

"I don't see any need to wait for a dinner party to bring out my china," says Mary. Some of her summer whites, above, are displayed on a vintage wall shelf and a lace-draped pine mantel below it. Throw pillows covered in cool bed linens, opposite—one of Mary's signature touches—turn an armchair into an inviting seat for letter writing.

Within these broad seasonal "strokes," little changes strike like sudden shifts in the weather. "Half the fun of having an all-white house is that you can move a piece from the dining room to the bedroom, and it will work," Mary explains. Her secretary bookcase has served as a vanity in the bedroom and as a linen chest in the bathroom. Unattached mantels have been moved from the living room to stand as headboards in the bedroom. Even her daughter Abigail's crib, the front rail removed and the mattress lowered, has been piled with pillows to become a child-size sofa.

No piece of furniture has traveled as often as her grandmother's double-pedestal mahogany table. Mary painted it white as soon as she inherited it, and it has since held court in the dining room, stood against a living room wall as a collections table, and served as a desk in the study, its two long drawers filled with paperwork. "It's a wonderful buffet, too," Mary says. "I've had gingerbread men billowing out of the drawers for a Christmas party."

With each reincarnation of purpose and new place in her home, the table has been painted a quietly different shade—white with a drop of pink, white with a hint of green—so that the color caters to the season and the slant and quality of its light. "I had

"Half the fun of an all-white house is that you can move a piece from the dining room to the bedroom, and it works."

the fellow at the paint store teach me how to mix my own colors," Mary says. "Some days I go around with my brush just looking for things to paint."

Or she goes looking for things to move. "I'm always challenging myself to reuse my pieces and have fun with them," she explains. "You don't have to get rid of what you have to make a room look different. Just move your furniture or take a collection out of the cupboard." Of course, if everything is white, change is so much simpler.

To dress her umbrella table, opposite, with vintage lace, Mary sorted through her collections until she found a tattered cloth. She cut a hole for the umbrella and ignored a rip. "I just folded the cloth over so you can't see it," she says. For china, Mary mixed mismatched blue and white pieces; she gave the table a unified look by placing them on top of white chargers.

THE $400 FLEA-MARKET BEDROOM

Addicted to antiques shows and tag sales, Mary Baltz specializes in giving odd finds new lives. To prove how much can be done on a limited budget, she set off for Brimfield, the legendary Massachusetts flea market, and $400 later had the makings of the room shown on these pages. Instead of her usual white, she focused on roses. "It helps to have a theme," she explains. "It could be blue and white, stripes—anything that will anchor a room."

Mary snapped up odd lots of fabric with lightning speed. She found four yards of one print, enough to slipcover a wooden chair. Then she discovered three yards of another print for pillow shams and a vintage bedspread to layer atop a box spring to make a dust ruffle.

What to do for a bed? Mary found a gilded twin-size headboard and footboard—$25 for the set—and a few booths away lucked into bed rails that fit, $5 a pair. Back home, she treated the bed to White Dove latex paint from Benjamin Moore, then gave the frame a light once-over with Kiwi brown shoe polish on a soft cloth. "It takes the edge off the newness," she explains.

Mary's other Brimfield finds: a scratched mahogany side table, easily revived with a coat of white paint; a $30 mirror to hang in the middle of a window; and $1 milk bottles to hold clutches of freshly cut roses.

FROM CHINTZ TO WHITE

🅈 *Hollywood costume designer.
Nominated for Academy Awards
for* Bonnie and Clyde, The
Godfather Part II, *and* Peggy
Sue Got Married.

🅈 *Home base: The Cloisters, a
renovated cottage in Los Angeles.*

🅈 *Style signature: White floors and
ceilings paired with ever-changing
furniture and accessories.*

🅈 *Visual epiphany: The film
The Umbrellas of Cherbourg.
"I was staggered by the painted
textures—the peeling door and
lumpy paint. It changed my life."*

Theadora Van Runkle

Technically, Theadora Van Runkle is a costume designer,
translating meticulously researched sketches into silk and satin
realities. But first and foremost she's a "homebody." When she
isn't on location, she's in her art studio (a turret made from a
huge wine cask, accessible by a spiral staircase). And when she
isn't creating abstract oils, she's experimenting on the largest
canvas she owns: her white-raftered 1920s cottage.

In 1994, Theadora was in a paisley-and-needlepoint mood.
Her curtains were tea-dyed chintz, her antiques were dark and
sculptural. She has since been struck by "an overwhelming need
to get rid of all texture" and to simplify everything around her.

She painted nearly all her furniture white—"It's the most glorious feeling." Her brush ventured where few dare to go: She whitened the metal base of an antique Handel lamp, painted the carved spirals of two English candlesticks, whitewashed a cane-backed chaise, and even recolored a set of "very good" Regency chairs. "Some people couldn't believe I painted them," Theadora says. "But they can always be refinished. And I was *tired* of them."

Her next step was to recover all the furniture she owns. "I do the work myself," she says. "Upholstery is hard work, but it's all explained in books. I never thought life was really worth living if you paid someone else to do everything for you. You're not really at home that way."

What makes this life of perpetual change possible is a clean architectural background—a feat that requires more than a simple trek to the paint store. White thrives only with light, but Theadora's "nothing, absolutely nothing" bungalow was decidedly

With lace and pale striped slipcovers, opposite and page 105, Theadora transformed her living room. She abandoned her chintz curtains, above, and replaced the flame-stitched fabric on her three-corner chair with muslin. Some things remain constant: a white floor and hooked rugs, which she likes because she can wash them herself.

short on windows, not to mention architectural character. To remedy the situation, she brought in a SWAT team of carpenters to raise the roof—literally—and install a battalion of French doors so that every room felt like an extension of her garden behind the

"I used to think white was too luxurious. Then I realized that true luxury is something beautiful to look at."

cottage. When the sawdust settled, Theadora got out her ladder and painted the walls, ceiling, and floors the colors of clouds.

With everything white and simple, "life just seems easier and more fulfilling," she says. Hers is a high-maintenance life, but she likes the discipline it requires: shoes off at the door, daily dusting. "I have a reputation for being neat to a fault," she confesses. But this impulse isn't a Virgo-esque tick: Cleaning lets her hum about her house, appreciating its beauty, testing to see if any fresh changes are needed. "I consider it my closest and dearest friend," she says.

When she first began lightening
her look, Theadora faux-marbled her
antique oak table with pinks and
beiges, left. Later, when she decided to
go all white, she painted the table
again, keeping a hint of its black trim,
top left. This meant reaccessorizing, so
she got out her turned wooden candlesticks and painted them white, too.

Just as she does her own painting,
such as transforming her Regency side
chairs and antique center table,
right, Theadora tends her own garden,
opposite. "When you do things
yourself, you have a different eye,"
she says. Her own eye constantly roves
from house to garden, since all the
rooms were renovated to include
French doors that invite the outside
in—and vice versa.

FALLING IN LOVE WITH WHITE

"I used to think that white was too luxurious," says Theadora Van Runkle, long an admirer of 1930s British decorator Syrie Maugham and her monochromatic interiors. "Then I realized that true luxury is something beautiful to look at, no matter what the color."

Some have said there are thirty shades of white in her house. She has never counted. Each time she paints, she mixes a new tint. "It's important to have different shades so a house doesn't look like a wedding cake," she explains.

She begins with "a nice common latex" from any paint store. "Sometimes I add a little alizarin crimson to make it pink or meridian green and a tiny touch of yellow for dove gray.

If I want a room to look expansive, I'll use a cold, clear arctic white or mix in a little foggy blue to add a feeling of air. Occasionally, I'll add dust to get a lumpy pleasant look—I learned a lot of tricks in the movie business."

White, of course, may require a shift in accessories. "I love rocks and birds' nests and natural things," Theadora says. "And shells, though there's nothing madly original there. And I'm crazy about crystal because of the way it reflects light. Naturally, you can't put it against something impeccable. It has to be near something white but a little beat-up. Otherwise, a room looks too thought-out and it doesn't have any style."

EMBELLISHING A BUNGALOW

~ Interior designer and proprietor of the Dallas furniture and decorating store Room Service.

~ Home base: A 1940s bungalow in Dallas.

~ Training: The daughter of a builder, Ann has been playing architect since the third grade.

~ Style signature: Layers of color, texture, and pattern, carefully controlled so that nothing looks too romantic, too cottagey, or too contrived.

Ann Fox

"I love detail," says Ann Fox. "I look at a room and ask, 'What can be added?'" Not fuss and knickknacks but quiet touches—grillwork to embellish a corner, flea-market paintings hung above doors. Even the seemingly solid pink on her dining room walls is a complex creation. It began with textured wallpaper that looked like tooled leather scrolls with baby flowers. Then it was painted pale pink and accented with gold and cream, the latter colors applied with a rag and a paint pen.

Though such an intricate room would certainly encourage guests to linger, Ann doesn't take any chances. Not one for hard dining chairs, she likes soft-as-a-sofa banquettes. "When

I have a party, we don't 'retire' to another room," she says. To make the banquettes practical, she covers them in a collection of slipcovers, with patterns ranging from rose bouquets to white stripes. She rotates her prints just as she rotates her china collections, whitening for summer, brightening for winter.

Ann's taste for change has been inherited by her young son, Jackson. "As soon as the Christmas decorations are down, he insists that we decorate for Valentine's Day. I guess he's used to seeing my store change," she says. Fortunately, she designed Jackson's room for display, topping bead-board walls with a high shelf: "In some parts of the room it's just two inches deep, in other parts six." She showcases everything from paintings to Jackson's collection of outgrown cowboy boots. The chest at the foot of the bed was once the base of a vanity; it now holds sports gear. Ann says, "I love finding old pieces and thinking, What can we do with that?" The answer is, in her hands, just about anything.

Son Jackson's bed, opposite, with its nest theme, was painted by Ann's friend Jane Keltner. Its robin's egg blues were borrowed for the striped curtains. The top of the valance is flush with the ceiling, making the windows look larger. With so much white on the bead board, Ann didn't want a white ceiling, so she used a blue two shades lighter than the blue above the shelves. The floor, like that in the living and dining rooms, previous page, is pickled to keep the scheme as light as possible.

"Small houses," says Ann, "are great if they have nice kitchens and baths." This bathroom, left, is part of an addition. Sheltered by trees, it doesn't need curtains for privacy. "Besides, I hate hiding the moldings," she explains. The stars in the rafters, above, were traced using a cookie cutter; coordinating bracket shelves on the walls keep perfumes and supplies within a bather's easy reach.

Space, Cleverly Used

Present a designer with a tight corner, and watch the

creativity fly. No room for an office, for guests, for a

crowd? This is the sort of challenge that brings out

ingenious solutions and provides invaluable lessons.

Sheila Bridges

- ✐ *Interior designer and owner of Sheila Bridges Home, a shop in Hudson, New York.*

- ✐ *Home base: New York City.*

- ✐ *Style signature: Order and symmetry: "I love classic shapes and forms."*

- ✐ *Stress antidote: "Light colors are key for me—they help to evoke a feeling of calm and serenity."*

Sheila Bridges' decorating clients are bankers, music moguls, and movie producers. Her home—in Harlem's Graham Court, the beautifully detailed apartments built by the Astors in 1901—is also her office. For years she hosted meetings in the living room and used her laptop on the dining table while two assistants handled the phones and faxes in a spare bedroom. Finally, she decided she needed her own workspace.

The solution was to turn a storage room packed with inventory into an office that could double as a guest room. Sheila's design scheme began with an antique painted Provençal desk. It had an ample surface for spreading out drawings and

Nothing in Sheila's apartment is an idée fixe. When clients or friends visit, the designer turns her cane-backed desk chair, above, to face the daybed, opposite and previous page, and draws mustard-colored side chairs into the conversation. For serious solo work, she plugs in a laptop and phone at the desk. She chose the bookcase, opposite, because of its manageable scale—"I keep moving it from room to room."

swatches, drawers for squirreling away notes and plans, and a café au lait color that would look perfect with the khaki she envisioned for the walls. "I like my workspace to be very light, with a neutral palette," she explains. The colors in the rest of the apartment run from apple green in the dining room to a dusky blue in the bedroom. But even at its boldest, Sheila's style is disciplined.

Such order and elegance cannot be accomplished without a few underlying rules. Sheila's a stickler for order and symmetry: pairs of chairs, matching bookcases, crisp window treatments like Roman shades. "I like furniture with graceful lines and workmanship so that you notice one thing from afar, another up close," she says. Her twin coffee tables, both with a funky flea-market pedigree, have ballerina-like cabriole legs to admire across the room and carvings to muse on at close range. And her caned daybed, an airy alternative to an upholstered sofa, was chosen because of its combination of intricate carving and simple lines.

PLUSH MINIMALISM

What makes Sheila Bridges' look so interesting is that it is both pared down and plush. There are pillows to sink into, velvet chairs to rest on, and curvaceous furniture to admire, but the designer is a minimalist at heart. She doesn't overstuff a space: Why have a sea of seating in a living room that's generally inhabited by a Jack Russell terrier and one or two guests? Why have an office as crowded as a conference room when you usually work alone?

Sheila designs for intimate conversations, then positions pairs of chairs, like the one shown on the opposite page, on the perimeter of her rooms. In the hall and dining room are additional seats, waiting like well-mannered dance partners for their cue to join the party.

Predictably, Sheila doesn't have much patience with knickknacks. Her greenery is sculptural—tabletop topiaries, flats of grass, bunches of grape hyacinths, a single orchid—as are her accessories, primarily ceramics chosen for their form rather than their collectibility. "I'm always interested in the silhouette, in the shape of things," she says, pointing to the arc of a tulip, the line of a lamp. She likes to give objects room to breathe: a single painting above a daybed, an understated assortment of ceramics on a bookcase. Room for the eye to wander is essential to the feeling of peace and serenity that Sheila is so adept at creating.

~ **President and general manager of the Waverly Group.**

~ **Home base: New York City and Connecticut.**

~ **Style signature: Neutrals with lots of texture and a touch of red. "My personal taste is very simple—pure lines and things gathered from my travels."**

~ **Bon mot: "Life is a collage of people and ideas. And that's what makes a home interesting."**

THE WELL-DRESSED ROOM

Christiane Michaels

"People aren't afraid to put clothing together," says Christiane Michaels, "but they lose confidence when it comes to the home. When visitors come to your house, they should feel as if they know you. I always talk about how you don't decorate a house; you create a rewarding, fulfilling environment."

One way to begin is to look in your closet. "In summer I love to wear a white linen suit and red shoes—I feel happy all day," Christiane says. To convey that mood with fabrics and furniture, she gathered tearsheets and swatches and composed an idea board. "It's wonderful to clip and pin and watch a story emerge," she says. In the rooms pictured on these pages, the

In this small white apartment, pattern comes from a variety of accessories— throws and books, opposite, and the pillows, baskets, and ottoman, previous page. On the shelves, above, old volumes are turned spine-side in, creating a striped effect, Christiane's simple way of giving bookshelves a fresh look.

story is deliberately simple. She chose white for the walls, linen for the love seats, and sea grass for the floor, creating the decorating equivalent of her white linen suit. Then she added touches of red as one might add bracelets or brooches, covering pillows and an ottoman in exotic prints—figures from Persian miniatures, patterns copied from Oriental rugs.

These fabrics come to life in a room punctuated with souvenirs from Christiane's own journeys. "I travel all the time, and I'm always bringing home something from Turkey, Italy, or France," she says. "It's important to display your treasures. The things that tell your story—these are what make an interesting home."

As someone with decidedly peripatetic interests, Christiane doesn't surprise when she proclaims, "I love change." She conceived the living room as a beige-and-white canvas colored almost entirely by accessories. "I'm always falling in love with the latest prints at the office," she says, knowing full well that a new parade of pillows and a

slipcover for the ottoman are in her future. "When I was growing up everything was altered with the seasons," she says. "Couches were slipcovered in the summer and layered with shawls in winter." She has designed this apartment for change—of accessories, fabrics, and even furniture placement. Dining chairs can migrate to the living room for extra seating; in summer, the love seats can be turned away from the fireplace and toward the windows.

But there is one immutable: a red dining room. Even though no other color makes candlelight so glamorous, red was a bold move in an alcove space, footsteps away from the creamy whites of the living room. Christiane knew that switching decorating octanes would make all the difference. "Red," she says, "makes a small space come alive. You have to choose your color carefully. Nothing too bright, nothing too demanding—it has to feel like a neutral."

For the red walls of the dining room, opposite and above, Christiane selected a Waverly hue with all the weathered calm of an old barn. Fabrics are smartly neutral; interest comes from texture— the contrast of sea grass and matelassé slipcovers ("laundering makes the pattern bloom") with button fastenings.

BLUE-JEANS EASE

Edwige Martin

- *Advertising art director who moonlights as a textile and wallpaper designer.*

- *Home base: Paris.*

- *Style signature: Stripes and denim, borrowed from her weekend wardrobe.*

- *Cross-cultural observation: "The American home is very—I don't know how to describe it—very natural and easy living. We don't have that in France."*

- *Bon mot: "Denim is classic—it's never out of fashion."*

"When you take a pattern that you wear and put it on the walls, you see a room in a different way," says Edwige Martin, a Paris designer who has translated the look of blue jeans worn by "every French teenager" into wallpaper designs. The stripes are trompe l'oeil seams, rumples and all. Denim "can be casual or elegant," says Edwige, whose wallpaper works equally well in chandelier-lit rooms and tiny flats, like her own apartment in the artistic Bastille neighborhood.

Her own furnishings, which were mostly gathered from Paris's famous flea markets, are as versatile as her textile designs. She likes wicker café chairs because they can go from the living

room to the kitchen and back. An old painted bench is both coffee table and extra seating—"Old furniture is easy to live with," she insists.

So, too, are her patterns. "Plaids, checks, bandanna prints—they're casual and confident and don't take themselves too seriously." But as much as she loves her wallpapers, actually pasting them on the walls was a leap. "Before I designed this collection," she admits, "I would never imagine putting a pattern on my walls." And not because Paris apartments typically have high ceilings and beautiful architectural details. "I think the reason has to do with culture," Edwige says. "Wallpaper is English and American, not French."

Edwige learned to appreciate the possibility of pattern a decade or so ago when an advertisement in the *International Herald Tribune* landed her a summer job as an au pair for decorator Lyn Peterson, the founder of Motif Designs, a wallpaper and fabric company (see page 32). Edwige minded Lyn's children, and later Lyn minded Edwige's career, producing her designs.

Edwige approaches decorating like tablesetting—mixing patterns on the sofa and walls as she would placemats and napkins, opposite and above. She even hung a painting on a curtain, page 137, positioning it as if it were a tray on a tablecloth. Stripes and checks are wonderful," says Edwige. "You can mix them, as long as you keep to a similar palette and a similar scale."

"Patterns that are crisp and simple go with all sorts of furnishings," Edwige explains. *In her bedroom she has paired her denim-stripe wallpaper, here in a stonewashed blue, with the scrolling lines of a flea-market headboard. A tall mirror in the corner and a bull's-eye mirror on the mantel give the room new perspectives.*

Even after a full day at an advertising agency, Edwige is still inspired to work on new fabric designs, sketching at her home office and dreaming of translating more everyday fabrics— patterns from lawn furniture and hammocks, for instance—into designs for the home. Here her bandanna check covers the walls and a simple blue gingham decorates her work surface. A ribbon board lets her display her latest inspirations.

Drawing on Tradition

~⚬~

The tinkle of crystal chandeliers, the curve of an

antique roll-armed sofa, and the feel of rich tapestry.

Is it possible to love the past and live in contemporary

comfort? Yes, these rooms reply, most certainly yes.

COMFORT IN HISTORY

Joedda Sampson

ℐ Historic preservationist in charge of eighty employees at Allegheny City Restorations in Pittsburgh, Pennsylvania.

ℐ Home base: Her latest rescue mission, the eighteenth-century Gwinner–Harter mansion in Pittsburgh.

ℐ Style signature: Period pieces used with a consideration of contemporary comfort.

ℐ Bon mot: "If you look carefully, you can find lots of Victorian chairs that make you want to sit down with a cup of tea and a novel."

If there's a wrecking ball about to swing in Pittsburgh, Joedda Sampson is more than likely to be there, waving her arms and yelling "Stop!" In the last ten years she has rescued seventeen historic houses, including Victoria Hall, the house shown on these pages. Owned by the Knights of Columbus for seventy years, Victoria Hall had acquired an unfortunate institutional look. But Joedda saw beyond the fluorescent lighting and became determined to restore the once-grand house for herself. Though she has since moved to another work in progress—letting Victoria Hall earn its keep as a bed-and-breakfast—she is still immensely fond of the house, largely

because the décor illustrates an approach to Victorian style that she has fine-tuned over the years.

"The first priority of the Victorians wasn't comfort," Joedda says bluntly. Most parlor furniture, a Victorian house's "best" pieces, was meant for formal, corseted occasions. The gentleman and lady of the house often had more casual sitting rooms off their bedrooms. "That's the furniture I look for. In sitting rooms, there were great, comfortable wing chairs that wrap around you"—one now sits in Victoria Hall's parlor—"and sofas your kids will fight to sit on." Joedda found a Second Empire mahogany roll-arm sofa that's "probably the most comfortable sofa in the world." To enhance its inherent coziness, Joedda overstuffed the seat and back—after she removed its original, "horrendous" velvet—and covered it with a serene stripe.

After seating, Joedda feels that the most important element of a Victorian room is lighting: "If it isn't right, a room is like a

Beneath a suspended ceiling in the dining room, Joedda discovered the original cove molding decorated with embossed leather, opposite. Missing pieces were replicated in plaster. Her table and marquetry sideboard are both Art Nouveau. For reading lights, above and page 147, Joedda believes in refitting period fixtures.

woman without jewelry." Joedda's rooms wear the decorating equivalent of diamonds: gorgeous chandeliers. "Venetian glass is my absolute favorite. I love its opalescent quality and myriad colors," she says. "I also like a lot of torchères to play up high ceilings." For

"I worry more about decorating than about furniture. Rich curtains and carpets, beautiful chandeliers—those create romance."

Instead of coffee tables, Joedda relies on parlor tables like this oval one, opposite, decorated with enamel and papier-mâché. "If you use little tables cleverly, at the end of a sofa or next to a chair, you can get away from having to have something plunked in front of the sofa," she says. The walls are covered with paper that resembles green brocade. The library beyond is fitted with bookcases that were bought at an estate sale.

reading light she uses electrified stained-glass lamps. She counteracts the darkness of much Victorian decor with "a lot of mirrors and sconces. You can't be a vampire and live with me."

Last on Joedda's list of decorating priorities is curtains. "Mine are probably kind of fussy. I like voluminous drapes pulled off to the side with tassels. People look at the curtains and say, 'That's really something.' All it is is fifteen yards of fabric, but that attention to detail is what creates the ambience of a Victorian room."

STYLE ON THE MOVE

Nina Campbell

ᴊ᷒ *Interior decorator, fabric designer, and author.*

ᴊ᷒ *Home base: London.*

ᴊ᷒ *Style signature: Upper-crust English country style, suitable for clients like the Duchess of York, as well as being welcoming to children and dogs.*

ᴊ᷒ *Bon mot: "I'm trying to debunk the prissiness of decorating. Interesting, comfortable rooms needn't be fussy."*

In the last decade or so, Nina Campbell has called at least three London houses and apartments home, and her decorating look has traveled beautifully from location to location. "In England you just don't throw out furniture," she says. What doesn't fit—a huge family portrait, two elaborate chairs—she puts in storage. But, she cautions, "you have to keep a pretty beady eye on what you store. Otherwise you'll end up paying more for storage than the things are worth." She recommends photographing rooms before a move in order to keep track of what you have—she's still looking for the chest missing from a pair—and plan what will go where in your next location.

"Having furniture from a previous home is very comforting," she says. "After all, those pieces are old friends." A new house affords a chance to see familiar furnishings anew, perhaps in rooms with different purposes. "Always try pieces you are unsure about," she

"I love decorating with red. Elsie de Wolfe said you should always have a red chair because red makes shy people feel better."

advises. "It may be that the large chest you thought so intimidating will make a tiny room appear bigger than it really is." Her basic guideline: "Put everything you own where you think it should go, then begin to weed."

One thing that almost always needs weeding is lampshades. "After five or six years, they get a bit dirty and dusty," says Nina. "Besides, it's time for something new"—maybe a triangular shade or red checks, something that will shed a new light on your old decor. She also recommends rotating collections. Currently, her

On one side of the living room, a fabric-covered screen, opposite, hides a radiator. "I could have done a box, but this looks nicer with furniture in front of it," says Nina. At the fireplace end of the living room, page 153, Nina placed a pair of red sofas and an upholstered fireplace fender that seats six. Walls are covered in linen damask, and the same fabric is used for the curtains.

Nina has a rooftop deck, a rarity in London, complete with a market umbrella, *above*, that she lined with a dark-green check. Her conservatory is sheltered from prying eyes by matchstick blinds on the ceiling and voluptuous curtains, *right*, at the windows. For dinner parties, she places a low blue-and-white screen across the kitchen door to block views of the sink but allow light into the room; cupboards house amethyst glass on the terrace side and a washer and dryer across the room.

monkey figurines have migrated to the bedroom, though one stray remains perched on the drawing room mantel. And her china collecting has shifted from the blue and white she still displays in the kitchen to the amethyst hues now seen on the conservatory table.

Of course, with any new house, new purchases are necessary. For the drawing room of the airy London flat on these pages, Nina bought new sofas because she needed to have a pair, then added a cushioned fender around the fireplace for additional seating. In the conservatory—what she calls her daily dining room—slipcovers enabled her to bring in chairs with "far grander fabric" from the library and blend them with her blue-and-white color scheme. "Such touches of continuity are important," she says, "whether you are moving into a new house or simply redecorating."

Daughter Henrietta's bedroom, opposite, opens onto the green of the ivy-clad terrace, above. Nina thinks of it as a tree house, light as a cloud, with linen on the walls, a white tablecloth for a bedspread, and muslin for curtains. The wall of pictures includes dog paintings that once hung in Henrietta's nursery. Nina laid them on the floor, puzzled out the arrangement, and then began hanging.

- *Interior designer and author.*

- *Home base: New York City, East Hampton, and Aspen.*

- *Style signature: English formality paired with curl-right-up comfort.*

- *Guiding influence: "My father, who always used to say that observing doesn't cost a dime."*

- *Visual advice: "Look carefully at decorating magazines. You have to read them over and over. Clip what you like, make files, and educate your eye."*

MASTERFUL SOLUTIONS

Charlotte Moss

"Decorating is about problem solving, not just pretty fabrics," Charlotte Moss likes to say. An air conditioner gapes in the wall? Hang a large painting over it. Pipes frame the window? Extend the curtains to camouflage them. But those are merely tricks of the trade. The real genius of her rooms is in the way she solves the stickiest problem: just how a client can truly live well in a given space.

"We talk until I have something to hang on to," says Charlotte. "Maybe the word 'lush' will come up. I'll ask, 'Do you want to come in and see flowers?' If so, I'll use a floral print on the walls or curtains—when you walk in you see

what's at eye level first. If I'm hearing 'serene,' maybe I'll use a tone-on-tone stripe at the windows and limit roses to a pillow or two."

On the parlor floor of this narrow Georgetown apartment, flowers prevailed, but in a muted, tea-stained print that offers a reminder of the garden in the backyard. Since the windows lacked architectural character, Charlotte gave them presence with floor-to-ceiling curtains, concealing heating pipes in the process. But curtains so impressively scaled can take over a room, so Charlotte balanced their strong verticality with a horizontal dose of roses on the sofa and two Aubusson carpets with similarly toned florals.

Rugs define what at first glance look like living and dining areas. But instead of being designed only for times when candlelight sparkles and friends crowd the sofa, the space is meant to be comfortable every day. "My test of a well-decorated room is whether you want to sit down with a book and a cup of tea when no one else is home," Charlotte says. The living room's sofa—her own

Matching window treatments frame the dining area, opposite, and the living area, page 161. In the absence of guests, the dining table is positioned by the garden window and set up as a desk. Paintings and framed photographs help obscure a metal grille. The fabric-covered stationery binder, above, is made with patterns designed by Charlotte.

Charlotte calls her book-binding red sofa "the line of demarcation" between the living and dining areas. Touches of red dance on either side of it—in the stripes on the chair and in the velvet pillows on the floral sofa, page 161. She likes to leave books open on the ottoman she uses as a coffee table. "Whenever you fluff your pillows, turn to another page," says Charlotte. "That way your accessories are always changing."

design—has a high back—its tufted detailing rises above the pillow line—and a soft seat. Instead of a coffee table, she chose an ottoman, which doubles as seating. Here and there, diminutive chairs serve

"In decorating it's important to create comfort and elegance, but you should always have an element of fantasy."

as foot stools, book rests, and, of course, extra seating for parties. "Who can resist sitting in a little chair," Charlotte asks, "even if you're in a cocktail dress?"

In the dining room, instead of the expected hanging light, she relied on the intimacy of lamplight. When it is dinner-party time, mail and magazines are scooped up, the lamp goes in the closet, and the floor lamp is shifted to the left of the fireplace. The table resumes center stage opposite the fireplace, and the dining chairs scattered throughout the house are reassembled. "It's like the curtain going up on a play," says Charlotte. "Everything takes its place."

The longer you sit in one of Charlotte's rooms, the more you notice—a painting standing on an easel, above left, cleverly placed at sitter's eye level, or a miniature chair tucked by a table, left. "It's the small things that give a room personality," says Charlotte. A case in point: the red trim on the sofa skirt. "Trim works there because it separates the sofa from the rug and adds substance to the skirt. But the most important thing about trimming is knowing where to stop.

GETTING THE HANG
OF PICTURE DISPLAY

The question of what to put on your walls is quickly followed by others: How many? How high? Where? Over a sofa, Charlotte began with one dominant piece of art, a gilt-framed oil painting. To give the painting a sense of importance, she surrounded it with candle sconces that complement rather than compete. At eye level from the sofa she added a pair of antique silk tapestries so guests have something to discover. They are hung just below the main picture—"I don't like frames that are all the same height," says Charlotte.

In working out a picture arrangement, "the only way to figure out the right balance is by seeing how things look." Arrange everything on the floor before you hammer any nails. "There is a lot of spontaneity in the process." Originally she thought she would hang a trio of images in the reverse order, but at the last minute she realized that she needed to put the largest on top to balance the weight of the painting above the sofa.

"When a room isn't overstuffed with furniture, I like to fill a wall with pictures," says Charlotte. Above the fireplace, shown opposite, she surrounded a mirror with four botanicals, again avoiding geometric precision. The prints lag a few inches below the mirror.

Bookshelf

The following is a selection of books by designers and decorators featured in this book.

⁓

Rachel Ashwell
Rachel Ashwell's Shabby Chic Treasure Hunting & Decorating Guide (ReganBooks, 1998)
Shabby Chic (HarperCollins, 1996)
The Shabby Chic Home (ReganBooks, 2000)

Nina Campbell
The Art of Decoration (Clarkson Potter, 1996)

Katrin Cargill
Bed Linens (Clarkson Potter, 1998)
Creating the Look: Swedish Style (Pantheon Books, 1996)
Cross-Stitch: More than 30 Nostalgic Step-by-Step Projects (Thunder Bay Press, 1994)
Easy Country: A New Approach to Country Style (Bulfinch Press, 1998)
Fabrications: Over 1000 Ways to Decorate Your Home with Fabric (Bulfinch Press, 1994)
Lampshades (Clarkson Potter, 1996)
Painted Furniture: Making Ordinary Furniture Extraordinary with Paint, Pattern, and Color (Bulfinch Press, 1999)

A Passion for Pattern (Clarkson Potter, 1997)
Pillows (Clarkson Potter, 1996)
Simple Curtains (Clarkson Potter, 1998)

Tricia Foley
Having Tea: Recipes and Table Settings (Clarkson Potter, 1987)
Linens and Lace (Clarkson Potter, 1990)
The Natural Home (Clarkson Potter, 1995)
White Christmas: Decorating and Entertaining for the Holiday Season (Clarkson Potter, 1997)
Williamsburg: Decorating with Style (Clarkson Potter, 1998)

Charlotte Moss
Creating a Room (Penguin Studio, 1995)
A Passion for Detail (Doubleday, 1991)
The Poetry of Home (Boxwood Press, 1998)

Carolyn Quartermaine
Carolyn Quartermaine Revealed (Rizzoli, 1997)

Calling Cards

Rachel Ashwell
- founder of Shabby Chic stores and author
- Malibu, California

Lillian August
- textile and furniture designer
- Palm Beach County, Florida, and Westport, Connecticut

Mary Baltz
- decorator and editor
- Southampton, New York

Carol Bolton
- designer and proprietor of several shops
- Fredericksburg, Texas

Sheila Bridges
- interior designer
- New York, New York

Nina Campbell
- designer and author
- London, England

Katrin Cargill
- decorator, editor, and author
- London, England

Isabelle de Borchgrave
- artist and designer
- Brussels, Belgium

Tricia Foley
- editor, author, and designer
- New York, New York, and Yaphank, New York

Ann Fox
- interior designer
- Dallas, Texas

Anna French
- textile designer
- London, England

Edwige Martin
- art director and textile and wallpaper designer
- Paris, France

Christiane Michaels
- president and general manager of the Waverly Group
- New York, New York, and Connecticut

Charlotte Moss
- interior designer and author
- New York, New York

Lyn Peterson
- decorator, textile designer, and owner of Motif Designs
- Westchester County, New York

Carolyn Quartermaine
- designer
- London, England

Joedda Sampson
- historic preservationist
- Pittsburgh, Pennsylvania

Theadora Van Runkle
- motion picture costume designer
- Los Angeles, California

Acknowledgments

This book could not have been created without the generosity and cooperation of all the designers we profile in its pages. Our sincere gratitude to them for allowing us to visit their homes, studios, offices, and shops, and for lending their time to be interviewed. Thanks are due to Claire Whitcomb, whose knowledge of home furnishings and design and whose incredible skills as an interviewer have brought the views of these women to life. Thank you also to the photographers whose wonderful pictures allow us to tell such inspiring stories and help us to learn so much.

Photography Credits

1	Christopher Drake	60–65	Hugh Palmer	136–143	Christopher Dugied
2	Dominique Vorillon	66	Toshi Otsuki	144	Steve Gross & Sue Daley
4–5	Guy Bouchet	68	Toshi Otsuki		
6	Toshi Otsuki (top, third from top)	69–73	Steve Gross & Sue Daley	146	Steve Gross & Sue Daley
	Michael Skott (second from top)	74–83	Toshi Otsuki	147–151	Toshi Otsuki
	Christophe Dugied (bottom)	84	Michael Skott	152–159	Christopher Drake
7	Jacques Dirand (top)	85, 86	William P. Steele	160	William P. Steele
	Christopher Drake (second from top)	87	Michael Skott	161	Steve Gross & Sue Daley
	Toshi Otsuki (third from top, bottom)	88–91	William P. Steele	162	William P. Steele
		92	Alan Weintraub/Arcaid	163	Steve Gross & Sue Daley
8	Toshi Otsuki	94–103	Toshi Otsuki	164–165	William P. Steele
11	Alan Weintraub/Arcaid	104	Michael Skott	167	Steve Gross & Sue Daley (top)
12	Christopher Drake	105, 106	Alan Weintraub/Arcaid		William P. Steele (bottom)
14–21	Dominique Vorillon	107	Michael Skott		
22–31	Christopher Drake	109	Alan Weintraub/Arcaid (top)	168, 169	Steve Gross & Sue Daley
32–41	Toshi Otsuki		Michael Skott (bottom)	170	Toshi Otsuki
42	Hugh Palmer	110, 111	Alan Weintraub/Arcaid	176	William P. Steele
44–51	Jacques Dirand	112	Alan Weintraub/Arcaid (left, third from left, right)		
52, 53	Guy Bouchet		Michael Skott (second from left)		
54, 55	Andres von Einsiedel	113	Alan Weintraub/Arcaid		
56	Guy Bouchet	114–119	William P. Steele		
57	Andreas von Einsiedel	120–135	Toshi Otsuki		
58, 59	Guy Bouchet				

Index